Cline, Franklin K. R., *So What.* First Edition. Paperback. First printing October 2017. ISBN 978-0-9992103-2-1. Library of Congress control number 1-5829441791

Cover art by **Shaun Gaynor**

for Rachel
the so, the what

SO WHAT
sonnet

And now all the sports video games got
stories where some
prodigy gets hurt young and comes
back older. And wiser. And then he
wins the big one. And his success in the face of it echoes
the big longing we share.

And then in the game some
simulacra of the people who yell at each other on the TV
yell at each other on the TV's TV about it. And the real people
on the TV yell at each other about that. And
then equally real people in bars yell
at each other in disagreement about what the TV men yelled.

And all this borne from this
stolen land: the simulacra, the hurt, the yelling, the men, the protagonist, the comeback.

SO WHAT

One day you wake up and you're responsible for the world,
Ephraim says to me in the wintertime across the lake on
the phone. I tried to transmit my love for him to him

but I don't know. Over beers
brewed in Kansas City
Quamar told me about his thesis in Chemistry

examining chirality: he puts
his hands up to illustrate the concept of nonsuperimposable mirror images,
points at a spiral staircase we can see through a window

and says *like that*. We don't have the credentials
to go into the room with the stairs he's pointing at. Is it my fault
my iTunes plays only men when I put

my music on shuffle. The universal emotion
of the face
crumpling in anguish and

or confusion. Do the machines
we build reflect our own biases. I was named I think

for my great-great-grandmother, renamed

by/for the Dawes Roll. Lots
of non-Tsalagi
tried to pass as for the Roll. I was

working in the lab late one night. Quamar
and I went to the art gallery and it made
the sunset

we drove into going north on I-35 more urbane. My father
told me the history of my name and
I'm not sure I buy it. When the praises go up, the blessings

come down. Dad wanted to name me X. We live in a thieved country run by thieves
and I love buffalo wings. You never
liked that song until you heard it in a car commercial. Thesis, antithesis, synthesis. I

wore a hat that said KC on the front of it and CHIEFS on the back
to Company Brewing today. I am a fan of the Chiefs. Nikki and Ngoho
and I drank Jameson and talked about the end

of the planet, how it's all really boiling, how like dandelions we remain
active. *It is heroic to try to stop time*, Jenny Holzer tweeted. I told Soham and Siwar and Ghassan about how I cried

when the Royals lost the World Series and when they won the World Series; I felt
so empty when I realized I'd spent
all this energy rooting

for this thing I have no
impact on.
People take for granite what these soldiers go through on a everyday basis!

Someone I don't know wrote that on Facebook and someone I do know
sent it to me, thought I'd find it funny, and I do think it's funny
but I also know the sadness of it: the wrong word

signifies the hard wrong of the wrongs soldiers enact and inhabit. It's
getting harder and harder to figure out who
the joke's on. It hinges on land. Earlier

I had to use the thesaurus to find the word "credentials." I asked
Rachel for the word but she didn't know what I meant
but she knew what I meant. My doctor said

to get my heart rate up for 3 hours a week. I thought that that
was already happening on account of
this thumpy life.

SO WHAT

Every night while
we dream they work

to take something
away. While we're awake they're doing it too

while we're busy thinking
about what's in the crockpot,

how we will shred the meat
when we get home. Duriel

has a poem that asks
over and over *how much*.

Today's
newspaper

had two gun
coupons

inside. Dust's an

eloquent

way to
measure the passage of time. I'm

not afraid of dying.
I'm afraid

of the moments
before, this

one excepting. Do you
carry yourself with

A) A much less than average amount of fear

B) A slightly less than average amount of fear

C) An average amount of fear

D) A slightly above average amount of fear

E) A much more than average amount of fear

So What
643 S. 2nd St.
Milwaukee, WI
53204

Place
Postage
Stamp
Here

SO WHAT

The sun breaks
through the grey and shines on my TV and makes it

hard to watch TV. I'm calm. I'm comforting. I don't
believe in harming anyone who doesn't

deserve it and I have a pretty good nose for those who
would be the best beneficiaries. Who benefits

from America? Who benefits from denying
health benefits?

How do they look on the outside and the inside? Often I wonder
what it would be like to have more money, I wonder

about the lived experiences
of inanimate objects. Why do I let my fingernails

get so long? I have no idea where my shit
goes when I flush the toilet. How far underground does the pipe

go where my waste commingles with the neighborhood's

waste, and is that the closest I get with my

neighbors? Rod to the south is nice but he works
nights so I rarely see him. He's asleep

during the day; I don't think Rod is one
of the people working evil at night. He says

he works at a factory. When the aluminum thud
of his car door announces his 4:30 A.M. slam home

I awake to think how happy I am for Rod
to be home like me.

SO WHAT

Down the block when younger they
used to strap firecrackers to cats I guess
to assert dominance and some of them
grew up to be cops and most of them
didn't. I can't figure out how to install
the Tsalagi keyboard on my laptop
so I'm stuck using English characters
in my studies: utana, big; uweji, egg;
aditasdi, something to drink.

There is a tenderness
in the way they punish
one another, Roger Ebert
writes about
a documentary
about independent
wrestlers in
Lincolnton, North Carolina. I
believe very strongly in the beauty of
professional wrestling: the joy of one
man lifting another above his head
and holding him there so long time

warps and every second matters more
than usual. It's refreshing to have good
guys and bad guys and that's it, that's
why Rachel watches the crime shows:
she says it's nice to pretend sometimes
justice gets delivered.

Stone Cold was embroiled
in a struggle with his
boss, who had a fleet of cronies he
called The Corporation. So
often we
got to see a
good
old
boy
beat up his boss and then
drink like
four beers at once
and then
pour some more beer on his boss'
supine body
and we want to be
Stone Cold

but eventually we want to be the boss,
too.

SO WHAT
sonnet

I am so often disinterested
now especially as
they are trying to break
us apart I have become fatigued

I am not disinterested
in the breaking apart

There are so many reasons to be afraid
of people you know and people you don't and the sky

is pure like the cocaine Cam'Ron raps
about in my headphones or a Westbrook dunk

the sky is pure like a Westbrook dunk
the sky is pure like all the reasons
to be afraid of others

the sky's purity is a matter of interest

SO WHAT

i'm trying
to avoid
this dangerous
culture
of want

mercury it
seems is
always
in retrograde

it's all getting
jumbled

meanwhile i'm
telling someone
i don't remember

if they asked or not

about pastoral poetry

it describes the land
without calling it stolen

generally, I
mean

anyway
why write poems
about the land

it describes itself

SO WHAT

East on Riverwalk during the protest a woman
breast feeds her child. This over
and over. The child, the bridge, the mother,
the viewer, the breast, the
protest. We will never make
a baby. Xavier covered
the spread but I didn't
bet on them. I said to C,
"Xavier is going to do this!" She
just wanted to get high I think. I keep having dreams I'm driving on
a highway in a car. Matt murmured you
like rental cars we slid into Chicago in the rental car
and I said yeah dude this is America
it's all a rental

SO WHAT
sonnet

Today cloudy our cats afraid of sky's big
booms I paid for a movie where men fight
over women I took off my shoes in the theatre put my feet
on the aluminum rail in front of me there was no one around

I felt free like the sky although the whole point
of a movie theatre is you cannot see
the sky although there were plenty of skies on the screen over
the course of the movie

Today cloudy earlier in a bar
a woman getting a divorce insisted I get another
she bought my second drink she still had
her ring on a pair of shoes sitting on the floor
can be so morose the radio exhales
while you drive and it's so your life

SO WHAT

Tonight the Royals

                                        play the Indians
                        and if
                                                they can sweep

                        them they'll
                                                                                be a
                coulplethree

                        games back

                                        in the AL Central

A cold front moves itself across Milwaukee lingering
like a bad thought

                                                        One of the cats
                                                took a shit
                                        on the mop
                        I was out
                        at the resale shop
                looking for clothes I

could rebuy

The shit ruined the mop

I hope the Indians lose

tonite we already lost

what's another series

SO WHAT
villanelle

The window's open so we blast our love out there
into empty took America
filling up. The sky so small but everywhere:

I don't want to talk about Jesus! I just want to see his face! Beware
of talk like this that doesn't rhyme when it could.
The window's open so we blast our love out there.

Sometimes the umpire's count's unfair
to the pitcher who's tossed ~90 ~90-mph pitches for
(the sky, so small, but everywhere)

6 2/3 innings and they disagree and the catcher forms a barrier
before fists clench and cramp. I never met a Veronica.
The window's open so we blast our love out there.

The stolen sky's okay but grey and bare,
silent yet sonic, a
sky so small but everywhere.

Mesh on the windows to make sure all but the smallest stuff stays out there

or remains in here. A windows-down car drives by blasting Metallica.
The window's open so we blast our love out there.
The sky so small but everywhere.

SO WHAT
love sonnet

Homebound in the passenger seat
     of the car at dusk, signs in the trunk, Rachel
steering home. Us in love despite the gloom
     fading in. Rachel wearing yellow
to bed amongst the cats fighting. I gotta finish
     this poem before she sleeps
so I can read it to her. Our
     apartment is warm. There is no one
filming us or yelling at us. We prefer that. Water comes with ease
     from the faucet. We cannot see our breath. Our trash gets picked up
on schedule. I'm so in love I walk into glass doors and don't
     bleach my whites despite the gloom. Rachel
your museum-bound lungs
     oh! Snatched away in the night.

SO WHAT

Who do you love? I
        meant to start this poem eloquently
           with an allegory
        but I told Freesia and Anja
about it
           and now I can't tell it
        again. The football games
           are over. Thousands
        of us are still drunk,
angry at the finish.
           We didn't play,
        but we cheered and are mad
           our team lost. Or they won
        but just didn't play good enough. 10,953
white boy blues bands played "Who
        Do You Love?" this weekend to indifferent
           patrons in the continental United States. I smile at everyone
        now because you never know. Few
smile back. It's tough to not be
           a wreck, it's tough to not be. I read the newspaper
        and then I rip it up and put it in the compost. My drinking
           is killing me. It snowed the first time this season

Saturday morning. I woke up and looked out the window
and saw the snow on our car and thought
about cleaning the snow off our car.
I remembered all the times I've cleaned
snow off of our car. What is your
identity, what is your
politics. Will you be okay. How do your babies
look. I would've been
a bad blues singer because I can't
sing. I have some kind of the blues; it's in the air, molecular:
blues singers take
what's in us and put it
outside of us and then we
got to put it back in. I park the car
on the land which was
stolen. The Chiefs lost to the Buccaneers 19-17
so I put on my shirt for the Thunder.

SO WHAT

The Royals came back from a 7-1 deficit! Moose shellacking a two-run
homer making it 9-7! Before
the evening I got
high and read *Lunch Poems*! We are dying! The sun
spread its pink fingers! Rachel and I went to dinner
and there was a wait so we got a drink
across the street! Anytime anything
negative happens to a person in power they deserve
it! It
was happy hour! Somewhere
an animal killed another animal! Meanwhile
we bought groceries! The earth,
slowly heating beneath our feet, yolked
us together! Gunshots! I played records all day
amongst the cats fighting! Now
the lights are on! I pulled off
the curtains in the living room cause I don't like them
and Rachel put them back up
cause she likes them! The Warriors
might sweep the Cavaliers! It
is all stolen! I haven't
shoplifted in years! I miss it! I'm in love

and it's accumulative
which makes it exponential
which makes it!

SO WHAT

Satisfied with the cooking shows
keeping me stupid, I heat

the coffee back
up to a nice warmth to match

the heat of the day so
I can feel like I'm drinking

the weather. I've put
it all into a cup and can

control it. The sun peeks out
through its sky and the sky doesn't

do much
of anything, which I envy. I asked for a beer

at a restaurant but they didn't have the beer
I wanted so I got

a different beer.

I'm discovering

new products at an alarming rate.
I'll not ever invent a new

product, never apply
for a patent. It's nice enough to

where I could open the windows but
perchance a touch too humid so I use

energy to keep the room my
ideal weather. And now clouds

float over the sun and mute its bright spray
and the TV tells me who made the best dish.

SO WHAT
because we come from everything

And the TV says ask your doctor if
your heart is healthy enough
for sex. The unpaid basketball team
is coming back to beat the other unpaid basketball team.
The game's tied up now with 2.1 seconds
left, but it's 2.1 seconds of game time
not real time. 2.1 seconds
is a long time at the end of a game. I migrate
across channels while
my blood migrates all through
my body migrating back into Tsalagi culture and language. I say back
because it so is not in. I hated
my Tsalagi dad so I resisted for a long time.

Everything is so beautiful: the view through our kitchen window
of our neighbor's roof I love and
the grass. Migration rolls around my veins and I wonder
if Rachel grinds her teeth in her sleep because
she married into migration.

My father: born from a bad fullblood woman who whupped

him good. I don't really know
if his mother is bad: when I met her we didn't talk much; her
third husband told me about life loading docks
and World War II and shit that I didn't
give a fuck about. That was my second time

meeting her ever; I wanted to learn. The game
ends spectacularly, a buzzer-beater to send
one team on and banish another. My father migrated
to Talequah only
after he burned Kansas City into ash, a trail
of debt and useless stuff and jokes.

Tsalagi post-push, we
were too thirsty, we took slaves, drooled
over land. It's embarrassing.
I am my father's son: I love to buy things: the awful rush,
the unforgettable sale, the looming.

SO WHAT

David and I walked home from Tracks and into
the evening part of the evening
we were so enraptured
by the awfulness of it
all and how we were so afraid and weak David is going
to ride the trains illegally again in August
which I support but am too scared
to do

My old apartment
in Kirksville had a big
garbage thing behind it I had to carry
my trash down the stairs I kept thinking
wow I should not have so much trash

I have a scar on my leg from when I drank
too much whiskey and cut my leg open
with a trash bag taking it down different stairs it will
always be there I think although now
that I examine it it has faded quite a bit it does not
make the impression it once did

SO WHAT

big wringer
all the killings
how little so many

wants
to say

against
but how big when of course so many
do say against

my reflex always is to say i don't know
like getting my knee whacked
or how the ground got so hard so quick
after the rain

it went down to 57 degrees

a big sigh i mean how else to keep reiterating
the stolen

and murder it just keeps going

on and on

i mean really

anything

the less they know
the better

today
i listened to a woman recite a poem
it was so true and beautiful she raised
herself up into
and became the poem

and i
never believed in anything more than everything
she said

SO WHAT
D.C.

Rounding the capital corner of 14th and Pennsylvania in Garret's Honda
there was a flash of a bar I thought
I was in Montreal the sky was pure
like a Westbrook dunk
I wasn't we linked arms facing away
from the White House and did the greatest
hits of chants I did not feel well after
Rachel said it was a good thing we
made people uncomfortable we made them listen
I trust Rachel but my opinion hasn't changed getting
high in Lafayette Square listening to Ross Gay read
Cornelius Eady's "Gratitude" in the shadow of the White
House man I texted Roberto
it was beautiful he didn't
respond that's okay he's not a hater I'm not
either I have done some haterish things but who
hasn't I recently learned
I handle a lot of liquor well and too much
liquor very poorly I am one train vibing past
woods houses car dealerships various
stories so many people afraid of people

they've never met

SO WHAT
sonnet

I wanted to get drunk
on the first day of Spring, manifest
myself as vanishing Indian and think about Rachel's
butt in her jeans but
it doesn't always work out that way. I stood on the curb
a moment and enjoyed how the Fugees echoed
out across Pierce from our apartment and
thought about wind and pages turning and time

passing. Whole generations just
zapped away by this place and the wind
keeps going, the cars keep clearing
their throats. Most everything's
already stolen; why not a few more hours
spent in it?

SO WHAT

We left town for four days and five nights and when we got back the apartment stunk. We couldn't figure it out. We tried changing the litterbox, flushing the toilets, taking out the trash, taking shots of whiskey, cleaning the fridge, reading books, fucking, inviting Peter over, side-eying the cops, feeding the cats, eating, not eating, sweeping, pissing, watching television, charging our cell phones, playing guitar, napping, making the bed, going to poetry readings, breathing, mopping, drinking wine, gardening, doing our taxes, getting into cards, going into different buildings, alphabetizing our records, scratching our arms until they bled, tipping our bartender, setting the table, buying more books, setting the heat at 69, using the Internet, washing our clothes, hanging pictures, taking out the compost, reading the news, crying over our dead grandparents, telling anyone who'd listen *there used to be grass here,* fighting, voting, taking the highway, rooting for the Kansas City Royals, dividing the apartment into halves, masturbating, talking about Palestine, vomiting, trying to figure out where to score coke, wearing scarves, protesting police, watching Westbrook hang 54 on the Pacers, paying rent, texting our friends pictures of the cats, yawning: basically everything we could think of. Eventually we were exhausted and we collapsed simultaneously on our queen-sized bed with the tender eyes of streetlights gawping as faraway sirens wailed, and we felt comfortable knowing those sirens were far away. When we woke up the smell was either gone or we got used to it.

SO WHAT
elegy for the Thunder's 2016-17 season

The night the Thunder lose to Houston in the first round of the NBA Playoffs 4-1, the night Russ goes 5-18 from the 3, the night I swear I'm not watching those motherfuckers cause I know they'll just blow it then watch the whole game anyway, the night overcome by clouds, the night I don't differentiate from dreams and whatever else, the night Rachel's mouth opens silently, the night I contemplate indigenous women's poetry as quilt, the night I wake up 3 AM and sit in Rachel's office and read Erdrich and think about noise, the night I yearn for and take one and then two shots of Rachel's good vodka to help put me to sleep, the last night Russ might ever play for us, the night I realize I yell for the Thunder more than I listen for thunder, the night cops report no arrests, the night like someone turned Milwaukee upside down and emptied it, the night it makes sense, the night night night thunder comes down.

SO WHAT
sonnet

One morning Spider
   caught a speck of lint
in her web.
   She interrogated it
and soon figured out it
   was not edible
but still kept it
   around. Later
that day, a caught fly, curious
   in his dying breath, asked
the spider, "What's
   that for?"
"Art,"
   Spider simpered, baring her fangs.

SO WHAT

Bubbling over with beauty sits Milwaukee doing its stolen thing
        Freddy and I wowed each other over
several beers and listened to a Jean Cocteau play read by Bergman and then

Annie came over and I asked her
        about how she moves
her lines around cause she has such weird indentions and it turns out

she counts the spaces she put up
        with me I had a beer at Company
Brewing and ran into Sky and Leslie

they're going up to the northwest
        this summer they're camping I said I preferred
the indoors I like the Internet and TV I like

to watch baseball Sky sent me the short
        film he made during the protests at Standing Rock I haven't
watched it yet I didn't go

to Standing Rock I am a bad Indian
        Deb Miranda taught me if the only good Indian is a dead Indian I am a bad Indian

I did five shots

at Dino's and ran into Freddy and went to Freddy's
          place as the temperature dropped into the 40s it was in the 70s the day
before but what are you going to do

SO WHAT

The tomato plants
in the garden aren't growing. I don't

know what we did wrong. Maybe
they don't get enough sun, there's

a lot of weeds on the east and west
sides of the tomato plants. The other

plants on the other side of the garden
are doing great. Rachel cleaned up

her side of the closet and now
my side looks like shit. I'm sleeping

better now that I drink
less. We've only

grown two tomatoes thus far and we suspect
the neighbors took one because now there's only one

on the vine. It rained real nice

today. I touched the soil before I came in

from work and my finger slipped
into the earth, which reminded me of sex. I don't have more sex

now that I drink less, which is not how it worked
five years ago. I have gotten more comfortable

with being in my underwear. I've gotten more comfortable
with being not afraid of dying. I'm afraid of

right before I die. I drink more water
than I ever have before. I'm reducing

my carbon footprint. I've decided
I want to be cremated and to give up my organs. I knew a girl

in college who died young and before she died
she raised a bunch of money online

and is now cryogenically frozen. Maybe death is how best to get
in touch with my body, with nature. I need

to sit in the garden,

not drinking. I feel so

uncertain, generally. I need to get my guitar restrung. I need to dust. LOOK UP 2017 NATIVE AMERICAN DEATH STATISTICS FOR TOWARDS END OF BOOK. Some damn squirrel keeps running around our walls. I'm glad it's found a home but I don't much care for all the commotion, especially when I'm trying to not drink and watch baseball and not be in the garden. The neighbors mowed off most of our watermelon. Does watermelon life begin at watermelon conception, the planting, the turning of the compost, the heat stink from when the lid fell off the compost bucket when I was taking it downstairs? Ah, it all devolves into argument. I used to be much louder than I am now. Old pictures of me not dead in graffitied basements, beer in hand, teeth exposed. The cats hide when it rains. Every day, death. So, hey: every everything, every every day. It feels good to be sweeping. We bought a new TV and I, distracted, lost its remote the next day. It doesn't have any buttons so it just sits on the designated TV table bookended by speakers waiting. Iliana said into her vodka the *I* was a big dick going at her face, every time she read a poem, then she won the AWP Donald Hall Poetry Prize.

We live in a thieved country run by thieves and I love buffalo wings.

We have agreed to never call the cops. The CHECK ENGINE light
has been on in my car for about
a week now. On in? I think so. I need

to get back in touch
with my body,
with nature. I walked

in the grass barefoot
but it just made
my feet itchy.

SO WHAT
sonnet after Ben Balcom's films

what hope to be gleaned from sitting together
what hope to be gleaned from light shielding darkness

what hope to be gleaned from all sitting same direction
what hope to be gleaned from not being able to talk to the person next to me

what hope to be gleaned from repetition
what hope to be gleaned from the gulpy aura of sincerity

when all else fails we go
to the movies

we popcorn
we feel the tilt

of the earth
on its axis

SO WHAT

Palpable dread now all over the silvery
slink of each day. We have been listening
exclusively to songs that feature real drums

and handclaps in order to remind ourselves
of the rhythm of humanity.
It's not really working, so we try

sex, which doesn't work any better but is
more fun. I don't know
if I can make it past my Caspers,

but I try at least a little every day. And, you know, this tarnished
land groans with every step anyway.
So I look up. There's a bunch of buildings and shit in the way of the sky.

SO WHAT

Please mail your answers from page 7, alongside any additional comments, to Var Gallery, 643 South 2nd Street, Milwaukee, WI 53204.

You can find various incarnations of these poems in *Matter*; *Forklift, Ohio*; "14 Possibilities of Native Poetry" from Connotation Press Online; *Red Ink*; *Return to the Gathering Place of the Waters*; *Eat Local / Read Local*; *Great*; *Wisconsin's Best Emerging Poets*; and *Resist Much / Obey Little*.

Within this book, you'll find interpolations of "Monster Mash" by Bobby "Boris" Pickett, "Blessings" by Chance the Rapper, "I Just Wanna See His Face" by the Rolling Stones, "Who Do You Love" by Bo Diddly, "Don't Fucking Tell Me What To Do" by Robyn, and "Knock You Down" by Keri Hilson and Kanye West.

Deep gratitude to the instructors without whose guidance this book wouldn't exist: James D'Agostino, Nancy Eimers, William Olsen, Brenda Cárdenas, Kimberly Blaeser, Mauricio Kilwein Guevara, and Rebecca Dunham.

Big ups and bottomless affection to my pals Glenn Shaheen, Laurie Ann Cedelnik, Brandon Krieg, Ephraim Scott Sommers, Iliana Rocha, Anne Strother, Garret Milton, Ching-In Chen, Lindsay Daigle, Tobias L. Wray, Mary Clinkenbeard, Soham Patel, Siwar Masannat, Freesia McKee, Peter Burzynski, C. McCallister Williams, Loretta McCormick, David Kruger, and Elias Sepulveda for the close readings, sagacious talks, warm support, and general eye-openings.

Thanks to my dear friends in the thread, for everything.

To Anne, Karl, and everyone at Woodland Pattern Book Center for leaking so much beauty into Milwaukee and beyond: thank you.

Love to Mom, wado to Dad.

Index

Franklin K.R. Cline is a PhD Candidate in English--Creative Writing at the University of Wisconsin-Milwaukee, an enrolled member of the Cherokee Nation, a member of Woodland Pattern Book Center's Board of Directors, and the book reviews and interviews editor for *cream city review.*